Rings in the Shingle

Images and Poems from the Norfolk Coast

Stuart Medland

Brambleby Books

Rings in the Shingle

Images and Poems from the Norfolk Coast

Illustration and text copyright © Stuart Medland 2014

A CIP catalogue record for this book is available from the British Library.

ISBN 9781908241160

Published 2014 by
Brambleby Books Ltd., UK
www.bramblebybooks.co.uk

Cover design and layout by Creatix Design
All illustrations by the author

Printed and bound by Blissetts, UK
FSC and PFSC accredited

Rings in the Shingle

Seashore and Cliff

To Isabella

Prelude

The concept of this book – the first of a series – is that of a random and personal choice of natural history subjects, mostly birds, to some large degree dictated by photographs that I have taken in the recent past and particularly like and that capture the essence of a wildlife encounter I have had. This kind of uplifting thing – or the possibility of it at least – is what a walk along the coast or over the heath or through a wood is all about for me. It is not intended to be by any means an exhaustive gathering-together of even the most iconic Norfolk wildlife species, although I have stumbled across one or two of those in my wanderings.

Rings in the Shingle is hence by its very nature an incomplete record – a life's work in progress – in that it relates to some of the more memorable 'chances upon' which I have had – and my response to that experience with a photograph together with the reflection upon it which resulted in my writing the poem. The inspiration for each poem may have come directly from the photo in question itself – its own intrinsic merits – so that the writing doesn't stray much beyond its borders, or the photo may have drawn me back into the encounter as a whole so that the poem spills out into the rest of the day. The photo is integral to the poem though and is not simply an illustration of it.

The idea for an accompanying piece of prose to give a little of the background to the photo and its subject came later in order to provide a balancing and relieving third element in the mix.

I hope it works!

**Stuart Medland,
Hindringham, Norfolk,
November 28th, 2013**

About the Author

A primary school teacher in Norfolk for much of his life, Stuart Medland has always written for children, and two collections of poems, *Pine Cone* & *Harvest Mouse*, published by Lark's Press, are from these years. Much of Stuart's writing results from his passion for natural history, and *Rings in the Shingle*, as the first in Brambleby Books' *Encounters with Nature* series, is a natural culmination and a happy fulfilment of this lifelong involvement.

His time is very much divided between the North Norfolk Coast and the Lake District about which he writes from a holiday cottage in High Lorton. A collection of his Cumbrian poems, *Ouzel on the Honister*, distilled from several decades' worth of visits and adventures, is currently in preparation. He is a regular contributor to the Poetry Journal *Agenda* with whom a book of poems in memory of his father, *Last Man Standing*, is also due to be published this year.

Stuart has a grown-up son, Dan, and daughter, Col, and has strong family connections with the West Country. He lives with his long-time partner Beth in the Norfolk village of Hindringham where he also draws and paints and continues to be fascinated and inspired by wildlife and the turning of the seasons.

Contents

Redshank

Author's Foreword

Half the author's proceeds from the sale of *Rings in the Shingle* will go to the CATS (Cure & Action for Tay-Sachs) Foundation, a charity set up in order to raise awareness of, and fund research into, potential treatments for the progressive neurological disorder known as Tay-Sachs.

Tay-Sachs is a largely un-heard of genetic condition caused by the depletion of a vital enzyme which results in nerve cells within the brain becoming irreversibly damaged, having often only just begun to develop. It is a particularly distressing and devastating disorder for affected families who will experience the happily normal development of a child only to witness the subsequent deterioration of all their senses and physiological functions as the lack of the enzyme becomes apparent. The condition may also affect older children as well as adults, dependent upon at what point the amount of enzyme in the system is no longer able to cope with the tendency of the nerve cells to go into decline. There is currently no effective treatment for Tay-Sachs.

This book is dedicated to Isabella, the four-year-old daughter of family friends, extraordinary (I would suggest, though they would disagree) for the devotion which drives them to continually explore new ways of communicating with their little girl as her faculties diminish, one of whose remaining enjoyments is the recognising of a CD of birdsong which she seems to respond to on a deeply intuitive level.

Hence Isabella's book – with so many birds.

To find out more or to help in any way, please contact www.cats-foundation.org

9

Ringed Plover

(for Dave Wood, Blakeney Point Warden, 2000-11)

How buoyant is she
on a shingle sea? She

Floats upon her every sense, her
eyes on the horizon so that

While this shingle wilderness
shifts all around her underneath
the crunch and infill of these boots,

Her head will keep its own position
relative to stars (just like
a Robin's in a windy tree, its body
swinging independently).

Just here, as well as anywhere, she
rattles out her anchor's chain; this
coracle of shingle for her eggs,
no more than someone's footfall-
divot in the rolling stones.

Her mask is hiding her from
possibilities; she weighs
not being seen among the
biscuit-bone meal
shingle by design

Against not being seen by
clodhopping mistake; by
human hoof as blind
to egg and bird as not.

Once, upon a Scottish Island,
we were standing at the
wrack-stripe limits of a beach
and toe to toe with eggs
without the faintest notion,

While we both delighted in
a plover, pebble-dashing,
zig-zagging its way between the
sea's weed and the stones
towards us 'til we gasped
at where she halted –
close enough for us to
hear her feathers as she
opened up her skirts to
sit upon her nest. It

Disengaged us
from our feet. I

Will return tomorrow, to the
shingle that my feet know best,
in all its vast and salmagundi
un-protection and I know

Already, I will find her gone.

Rings in the Shingle

Ringed plovers, related to Lapwings, are striking little shore birds, busy and feisty by nature and just about as ubiquitous (though not, perhaps, so busybody) as Oystercatchers. You can find them running about like clockwork, stop-start, start-stop, all over the shoreline shop and both sides of the shingle. It's most usual to come across them in ones and twos, but individual birds may well attach themselves to flocks of Dunlin, for example, through the winter months. In these circumstances, I've quite often seen a Ringed plover taking charge and being at the forefront of squadrons of birds flying low over the salt marsh mud.

Ringed plovers have the most unassailable belief in their own camouflage – their utility mushroom colour merging helpfully into shingle, sand *or* mud, and their

black and white mask doing a good job of breaking up their outline.

This bird had chosen to nest – if a shallow depression probably made by the heel of a walking boot, furnished with a wisp or two of straw can properly be called a nest – way out in the middle of a wide expanse of shingle created when the sea broke through the Shingle Bank during a storm one January night a year or two ago. The waves then evened it all out smoothly again to their own satisfaction.

I like this photo because of its clarity and the essential unwillingness to be distracted of the bird herself. She simply didn't move. As I inched forward on my stomach and then backed away every bit as slowly, she stayed trim and pert and confident in all her instincts. (I'm sure I felt far more

exposed than she did!) I was able to introduce a sense of distance, paradoxically, by getting good and low and foreshortening the shingle to a blur.

I desperately wanted to leave a 'Do Not Disturb' notice for her, knowing how difficult it is for even experienced and considerate walkers to spot a plover on its nest, let alone a dog let off its lead to bound joyously across the shingle plain with hardly a thought in its head. When I returned next day there was, of course, no sign that she had ever been there.

It is a consolation to me that this particular photograph, however, is being used as part of the National Trust's signage up on Blakeney Point, reminding everybody to watch where they – and I – are putting our feet.

Gulls Flare

(for Ben & Stephanie, whose chips they were)

Gulls flare and fluster
in the throwaway light of an
overturned paint-pot,

Day-dumped Sun.

Zinc-white and cat-call caught
in the long, slow cast of searchlight,

Scrambling the barbed-feather fence
of every other gull, unable to escape to

Drop the other side – losing
all their jelly-sandal footing.

Backlit by the mirror-flash of their own
wobbly baking-tray of sea, they

Swill a last-ditch tumult from its corners,

Seal the final documenting of it
with their softening candle-wax while

Bouncing, hot-foot incandescent
on the promenade rail – fused to a man;

The whole shocked flock – translucent
as the greasy paper for their evening chips.

13

Counting Out a Gull

Along this abacus
of promenade rail
(for doing sums and
separating out
the beads of
chocolate heads)

We only have
a single gull
abstracted
(neither added
nor subtracted).

All the other gulls
slid one way
or the other, up
and down the
seafront – destined,

Being seagulls,
to make ever bigger
numbers. Our gull

Is his own man –

Sticking to some
finger-clicking plan.

14

Promenade Gulls

The usual suspects, I suspect! Along with the odd *Cornish* seaside holiday Herring Gull, these are your 'Norfolk Promenade Gull' – the Black-headed variety; except that, in actuality of course, their heads are a Cadbury's chocolate brown – unless it happens to be wintertime when all they are left with is an unappetising smudge behind the ear.

Because it is such an obvious and popularly recognised seasonal plumage change, Black-headed Gulls are a great indicator of Spring on its way – or a Summer already gone.

The Black-headed Gulls in the previous photograph were squabbling for chips thrown by friends of ours who just happened to be sitting on a bench on a higher level of the promenade at Sheringham sea-front and were hidden from view as I went about grasping my own opportunity, so that I had no idea of the identity of the folk I had to thank!

It is the late Sun flicking its thumb through the gulls' flight feathers during the kind of chip-induced feeding frenzy which we have all been party to at some time or another – as well as the low light reducing the whole scene to a limited band of the spectrum – that is the key, I think, to the appeal of this photo. It is certainly redolent, for me at least, of a childhood spent in a similar seaside town elsewhere.

Meadow Pipit

Finds himself easily
Dotted and streaked
On the salt sea air –

Tumbled and
       squeakily-slipped
out of his grasses
           and fields on a

Crumble of cliff – to be

Wind-milling wings at the
Halting the slide of it
Down to the sea,

With his toes
On the half-snug
Round of a pebble.

All his hays and undergrasses, all his
     homely, seed-pipped earths, have
        finally agreed to let him go; the
          thought of them
             wind-tugging,
               nevertheless,
Over his shoulder,
    beating him, feebly
        with plantains. He

Skitters away,
    dancing his shadow
        out on the edge, thinking of
          changing his colours to
            stones and to sands –
Frisking their roots
    as he lets himself go,
        wise to the mineral slump.

15

These little birds are so easily overlooked, and yet their freshly-turned earth colours and grassy-seedy dots and dashes are exquisitely rustic and repay the closest of attention – which isn't that hard, especially up here where they are inadvertently concentrated and hurried along between the Sheringham golf course and the crumbling edge of the cliff itself by people out walking along the cliff-top path.

I love the bright, accommodating character of Meadow Pipits. They are quite unpretentious or even particularly wary, often skipping up to a fence-post just in front of you and seemingly disinclined to be the first to move on. They have the intuition to co-exist, except perhaps when in a flock and their inclination to be birds-of-a-feather is stronger.

Here on the grassy heights where the two species happily thrive, they put me in mind of mini-skylarks; their winsome song a more subdued and rarefied trill, their jinking, parachuting Spring display from nowhere near so grand a height as their more celebrated cousins.

These Meadow Pipits might easily be *Cliff* pipits or *Heath* pipits, *Moorland & Mountain* pipits – or even *Promenade* pipits, so widespread, so seemingly adaptable and eager to please are they. There are, in fact, Tree, Rock and Water Pipits (to name but a few), already recognised as different species, although these do display appreciable variations to the practiced eye. Perhaps, one day, there will be a Sheringham Cliff Pipit subspecies, at least!

I think the Meadow Pipit's almost cuneiform markings and its buoyant yet unassuming personality are well represented in this image. I particularly like the bridle looping underneath his cheek which nonetheless doesn't stop him looking round to see what's going on. The photo was taken – at very long arm's length – at the brink of the earthy-sandstone cliff which is constantly being worn and rubbed and beaten-away-by-the-sea to expose new stone and sand and soil… which are almost as quickly knotted together again by the roots of small plants. A ready and winning contrast of textures. There is a nice diagonal tumble to the composition, I think.

To the Coastguard Cottages

(Diary, May 30th)

Cliff top grass to the brink is wind-fingered shiny, squeaky-clean and Samphire-stretchy.

This is prime skylarking.

Upon a fence-post, light glows red and orange in a Meadow Pipit's legs; the Sun's juice drawn and threaded through a plastic straw.

He waits for me – in all his Perky-pip sobriety.

I am alive to details now; the epiglottal inflorescence of Angelica, behind him, is as paper-bag ballooning as the pipit's chest. What

Need of skylarks anyway?

Flint-knap Fulmar

Long-struck flint of Fulmar
    sparks the water –

Into blinks and glimpses
    of a mariner's tale,

Knaps each chalk-node roll of wave
    that turns clear out of sedimentary blue –

Chops it, hand-edge clean,
    to catch the light with several surfaces.

A Celtic cross lashed to a coracle with
    a stiffening wind across his shoulders –

Wheels at the cliff's falter, banking,
    (raising a Columban† eyebrow at us)

So the dip of one wing is the rising
    of the other – tooled planes of flight

Upon a chalky spindle –
    loosening the water into slips of slate

To make a landslide scree
    out of the Sea.

† A 6th Century A.D. Irish abbot and missionary who is credited with taking
Christianity to Scotland (where there are plenty of fulmars) and who founded the
famous abbey on Iona. The name comes from the Latin for 'dove'.

17

Tubenose

Sitting soft – his
Dodo's beak is

Heavy-duty
culinary and
artillery;

Swiss Army
snap-together,

North Atlantic
cable-snipper,
handy personal
filtration plant.

His, a thirst for the
whole of the Sea
to fire back its
salt at the Sun.

Nothing like a gull.
Only like an
albatross – its
egg beneath our
boating lake –
the Southern
Ocean's loss.

Fulmar Petrel

Fulmars are true seabirds, tubenoses like albatrosses, and as such are able to drink seawater and eject the excess salt through their nostrils. They are, also like their circumnavigating relatives, true masters of the air currents. Watch a Fulmar Petrel tipping the wind on long, un-yielding wings, clipping the cliff top grasses and then wheeling out to sea and round again in order to study you more closely, eye to eye – and any superficial resemblance to a gull, adept and acrobatic though they are – is quickly dispelled. Fulmars are also long-lived birds, and it is easy to impute a certain maritime wisdom to them as well as a genuine curiosity in their coastline neighbours.

I took a good number of photos of the Flint-knap Fulmar as it circled widely, riding the up-draught in front of me while I lay face down on the cliff top to catch the light in its sea-faring eye. The upper surface of its wings reminded me very much of knapped flints.

Only when Fulmars are struggling for space on a cliff ledge or chalky nest-site hollow is an element of inelegancy and comedy introduced – sometimes quite ribald and pantomime, as a male bird in this case, encouraged vociferously to get off its behind and do something useful about dinner, dances his way out into the face-saving seaside air.

20

High Seas

(Diary, August 31st)

Abetted by Moon as well as the Sun,
The Sea is at large this morning –

Magnificent with light and all its water.

Pummelling a fist along piano keys and
    generally china-smashing,

Kettle-drumming all along the coast
    from Sheringham to Weybourne.

Well, I keep my distance, wordlessly and only

Look out from the corner of my eye
    whilst keeping walking.

Dun sea rises and then arcs in rolled
    machine-shop bands of steel,

Sun-polished as it bends beyond its own believing and

Disintegrates into a knuckle-dusting, ten-rounds worth
    of blinding water-pebbles

Pushed too far.

The shoreline shudders and sighs.
This has gone on long enough.

I have the spray upon my bare legs
even this high up and you are higher still, a

Tiny living entity in such a
silver Neptune's trident, thrown
at-ear-and-elbow angle not to stall
and leaving your own wake upon the wind.

21

Washing-line Cormorants

Cormorants are a not un-common sight along the coast here though there are precious few places for them to stand offshore to hang their wings out to dry. The beacon-basket posts at the end of the groynes are quickly commandeered and popular perching spots for this reason. Then a washing-line cormorant may have the look of a Viking Raven or even, at a stretch of the imagination, a Roman standard-bearer's Eagle.

This bird was particularly close inshore, lost in its own thoughts possibly, as I was walking on the beach and lost in mine. I snapped out of my reverie in time and swung the camera round to follow him as smoothly as I could as he came by. I knew that out of half-a-dozen snapshots, one of them, at such close range, might well be in good focus. So it happily proved.

Cormorant

Cormorant passes un-
waterproofly by

On fingertips
that only hold on to his drips –

Determined not to
catch my eye
whilst

Looking for a handy
(groyne's end
beacon)

Place to dry

Sand Martins nest in monastic-cave-like communities of metre-long tunnels each with a nursery chamber at the end, excavated easily from the soft cliff-face and simply extended into the coastline every time the sand-soil slips to reveal a clean, new entrance hole.

24

Newly fledged youngsters will teeter on the rim of their intoxicatingly high and airy Brave New World encouraged by wheeling aunts and uncles to pop their cork – only to be duly returned for a toddler's nap before venturing forth to strengthen their wings yet again.

Having spent several days the previous summer photographing the Sand Martin colony between Sheringham and Weybourne – of which this photo is an example – I was saddened to discover, upon returning to the site one day the following March, that it had disappeared. A good metre's worth of the cliff-face had simply slipped away to the bottom, tunnels and all, after a week's worth of rain. It must happen all the time, of course, and the Martins will be life-lesson programmed by now to either start all over again without any fuss or shift slightly further down the coast to an abandoned site and maybe redevelop that.

I was quite affected, however, by the apparent disconcert of the first few young birds returning to find their birthing-holes simply wiped from the map, circling around and around, wondering perhaps whether they had, after all, been foolish to trust their inbuilt GPS first time back – despite what Mum had led them to believe!

On the Face of It

(Sand Hermits)

On the face of it
the cliff is vole-holed
as a riverbank,

Dry-canyon riddled
(to, admittedly,
another scale) with
hermit caves. Yet

However the face of it slips –

Shows even truer colours,
comes away with all the heavy languor
of a gym mat, slumping at the bottom, back
against its own wall, feet
towards the sea, however

Thick – or thin – the sections twice-removed by
thump of sea or loosening drench of rain;
slow-motion toppling headland,
flapping sheet of sandy soil –

A yard of ale of
Martin tunnelling

Remains. Each
lop of sand-pipe
only serves to
shove another
O Surprise of
bird hole to
the fore – the
next one in the
queue, like
pool balls
in a rack.

Dry sand puffs
at every blowhole
cell, back-pedalled
from un-sandaled feet.

Around my pilgrim head
a merry wherrying of
novices – brown

Sackcloth, spinning
sea spume white.

25

Sea Pies

Such familiar coastline birds; at home on rocky shores or shingle, sandy ones or mud. Ignoble, maybe – ignorable, never.

Oystercatchers (Beaky Billingtons, Sea Pies) are a noisy, busybody, in-your-face kind of bird. The interlocking black and white makes them unmistakeable but it is the orange-cum-red-cum-pink of the beak that fascinates me most (it's an amazing shade of colour to try to mix with pastel crayons, for example). That – and the crimson eye with its orange ring. Oh, and the knobbly pink legs that always seem too short to me!

I may have pulled those little Ernie Wise legs a bit in my description of a solitary bird, but Oystercatchers in a flock creating their own distinctly piebald horizon at the edge of the sea or, as here, taking to the air together, are a truly eye-catching sight. The fact that they rise as one and in silence adds to the drama for me.

I return to this photo again and again in order to wonder at the essence of their flying; the position of each bird's wing at any given moment through the rotation of a single beat – one bird's position in the air relative to the next.

This image is one of a great many I took out on the vast sand and mud expanse of Stiffkey Freshes where the Oystercatchers had found themselves scattered amongst a similar number of Dunlin in an interestingly regular manner (which would have made a nice wall-paper pattern) after an hour or so's lug-worming. They then rose as one just like iron-filings drawn by a magnet from a pile of wood-shavings – for example (sorry Dunlins).

Oystercatcher Liner

Oystercatchers lose themselves or not, without a problem.

Always happiest stretching a point – aloft and

Smudged lengthwise and high-tide accordingly, as
      sand goes meltingly into the sea,

Pulled by every long-pinched beak to make them
      water-eyed as any nose between the knuckles will do.

Noiseless for the moment and un-bothered, to be simply
      stripy as the sea and sand and sky, together-whatever.

Streaming black and white and red –
      they are a ticker-tape Atlantic steamship liner undertowing

All the dragon kites along Hunstanton Beach.

The feathers of their armpits mussel-hollow and their
      rock-pool wings grooved like a cockle shell.

Caught Out Dancing

(Diary, 10th March) In memory of David Stapleford

Blackthorn all a-spark
along the lanes out to the coast – an
eyelash-caught-under –
an-eyelid-prickling trail of
pop-magnesium that
carries me apace, a-fizz.

At Walsey Hills I am
pegged down by canvas-heavy
Greenfinches among the gorse,
too tightly-so to turnabout; a
flock full-twittersome, with
chiddling and with wheezing
(which includes a slurp I had not
noticed, at the end)

And at the pool-scrape,
Avocets returned from
open-all-hours estuaries,
hardly gone – but quick
to take the Spring shift
from the Golden Plovers
(no light for my camera is
good light for the Avocets).

I breach the shingle-shift
to find the sea surprisingly
up-close – and at its edge

An Oystercatcher
caught-out
dancing with a
starfish,

Rolling five-point
cartwheels with it
all along the tide line,

While a second,
mesmerised, is
staring at them –
pink, in every
arm and leg – and
then, again, at me.

It is a Saturday.
We meet up at the
'Dancing Goat'.
My good friend tells me
this may be our
last such Saturday
and as we talk and
laugh as we have
always done, I

Have to try to keep the
Oystercatcher and
the starfish
spinning

Round my head and
all along the coast.

For Wolves, Read Sanderlings

You'd laugh – and
be reminded of your favourite film
Dances with Wolves;

For *dances*, reading
chancing it a bit – the
sea already lapping at my heels,
my knees fast-sinking in a
pool of sopping sand
that makes a little moat.

For *wolves*, read *Sanderlings.*

In following these tideling birds
along the water's edge –
incoming with it, chivvied with it
swilled like dinner-
plates beneath the tap –
I'm caught out too

So that the Sanderlings have
quite accepted me as being
in the same predicament –
about three-dozen of us

(only one, admittedly,
entirely flightless)
stranded, drawstring-
pulled together on this
Buddha-stomach
island of the sand.

I have been fascinated by their
individual exchange-rate;

How they run on tiny
fire-tongs always
springing-back already and
so hand-to-mouth
there is no time for either
foot to touch the ground, so

Run-around, they'll run
around each other to be
facing in the right
direction for a

Power-shower nap, beak
quick-tucked under
wing for hardly
seconds at a time
before the rest have
gone and once again
it's catch-up time – all

Kicking-up the
pastry-crumble sand
into my stripy
deck-chair, beach-
towel happy lens;

For *dry*, read *wet.*

29

30

Sanderling Feet

Nothing gives the impression of running about in a blur like a Sanderling. Such quick-witted feet.

These are tiny shorebirds, forever dashing back and forth and in and out of the shallow swills of turning tide along the sandy stretches of the coast, usually in loose-knit parties, their beaks on the go all the time as if they were a myriad sewing machines. It is 'Knock-up Ginger' with the Sea – timed to perfection.

We see them in their winter plumage of soft whites and ghostly greys, smudged dark on the shoulders and edges of wings – and always those little black, liquorice feet!

The poem, I hope, tells the story behind the photograph. Just to re-iterate, however, that getting down low enough to come up with such an eye-level view has given me a healthy appreciation of the speed at which the tide comes in at this wide stretch beyond the Burnham Overy dunes, and how it very quickly searches out even the shallowest and most innocent-looking saucer-like depression to fill in around pre-occupied photographers!

The Little Terns

from 'The Blakeney Point'

The Little Terns are song-and-
dancing just offshore –

Streaming past me from the shell-crust sand
that turns into the proper, hard-won
Shrubby seablite-rooted coast itself, beyond

Its rolling rise. They like to fly

On jerky, undone-loopy, starter-handle
wings, their yellow-hanging beak
held on with an elastic-band which makes
a mask across their eyes. They do not
creak like Sandwich Terns who sound as if
they have a pile of gravel in their throats; theirs
is the last squeak of a bathroom window
that takes several pulls to close.

But they are flighty, hardly
sitting on their eggs for long enough
to do them warmth or justice.

I am at their roped-off nesting site. This is
a fine enchantment. How do merely ropes,
tied loosely between gardening canes
contain and strictly separate, both
keep and keep apart, when I could duck
beneath so easily? Have they become
(because no-one has *ever* ducked beneath)
the wobbly cliff-lip of a seabird colony
where Kittiwakes make nests on ledges
barely six feet from our cameras, while
knowing they are safe? We would not
fall for them. But I have fallen for these

Little Terns, tipped off their
shingle shelf by something like an
Oystercatcher's sneeze, yet not
recoiling from the water right in
front of me; they simmer in amongst
their yellow poppies, horned and
trailing roots to tie and stiffen-up
the sand and shingle into soil.

31

Marionette Terns

Terns, Sea Swallows – as far-removed from gulls, despite a very superficial resemblance, as sea-side chalk from cheesy chips – the Little Tern most eye-catching and eye-tossing of all.

Razor sharp, marionette and feisty, you think you have them in your field of view and then, all of a sudden, they've dropped right out of it with a single twist of salty spray straight down the plug. Out of the sea or creek again, silvery sand eel or not.

These birds were photographed on my way out to Blakeney Point, at the spot where they traditionally nest high up on a crunchy-sand and shingle rise but not far from the breaking waves at all. Often the early summer air is full of them here. It is the preferred proximity to water in the choice of their nesting grounds that is commonly the cause of a poor breeding season should inclement weather and high tides conspire against them.

Three Cold Knots

The Cold has it – it has
driven these three Knots in,
tame from the Sea,
dragging their feet
and weary with it, so

They stand about, not
knowing what comes next,
their beaks hard up
against some wall – the
rude sound of photographers,
even, dampened by the
wadding, shingle-packing snow.

Conversant with the cold,
they are nonetheless
reduced by it into
another size again –
puff-sleepy, hardly
managing to work the
slightly skin-warm air
around beneath their

Salt-and-pepper feathers.

Only here for the warmth
of the winter, anyway –
elbowed out from the
circle of the Arctic,
tripping over bigger and yet
bigger hoops of latitude –

They're wondering just how much
further south they need to go.

Three individually freezing birds
turned up here to rub shoulders –
for the lack of a heart
to their millions.

Cold-Worn

These three Knot were so worn-out and drained by the cold that they could only be bothered to put the slightest of distances between themselves and me, their photographer. Any more effort might well have proved an unwarranted expenditure of energy.

Such is the bleakness of the scene under a low sky of freezing mist that even the birds' winter plumage seems almost warm in contrast. I very much like the texture of the deliquescent ice, absorbing the liquid that will melt it.

That single drop of water trembling from the desperately dozing third Knot's beak is somehow so important to the effectiveness of this picture. A relief of tension for all of us. It is perishing cold.

Shingle Buntings

The shingle is at home among the birds, the
Snow-dip birds, the shingle; at a dozen

Shifting paces, one is
no more than the
other – twenty

Car-park spinning Buntings
potted in the dimpling
footfall divots of the
shingle bank

And nothing to be seen. One
whole flock melted –
winter-mixture mingled; flint
and sandstone, chalk and
heel-scuffed chalk again, into these

Countless tons of pebbles,

Drained, like colour from the cheeks,
at once upon their settling.

Work your way, frontline,
towards their disappearing
with your eyes, while knowing
that they simply must be there and

Still be, every single
time, surprised.

Buntings on The Shingle Bank

Snow Buntings, although so inseparably associated with the shingle bank at Cley and Salthouse, might just as well be Shingle Buntings – at least while they are here.

These are delightful little birds from the Arctic tundra that nest further north than any other finch or bunting, but see out their winter with us, hunkering down into the boot-heeled divots of the shingle slope during the very worst of our weather – the snow-flurried, salt-spray wind whistling just above their billiard-ball heads.

Most of the time, however, they are jinking along the bank up-and-down as if they are on elastic, tiny fairground horses on their poles, in smaller parties, going down the plug together to investigate the next horned-poppy trailing. Always in a changeover mottle of plumage, it seems, leftovers from last Spring, getting all spruced-up for the next in their white and their black – but always enough of the colours of shingle kept back to allow them their camouflage when they should wish; so much so, in fact, that you can easily stumble upon a napping flock, discreetly scattered, as you struggle seaward, to the top, before you have the slightest indication that there were any birds within a hundred metres!

I shuffled on my bottom up the bank to get as close as I could to this egg-cosy group of birds, keen to have at least one in some kind of focus whilst indicating how nicely and privately spaced-out they can be. The bird on its own I think is lit fortuitously but splendidly.

The Salthouse Snow Buntings, sometimes in the company of Lapland Buntings, are often enticed down to the car-park environs with handfuls of seed by photographers such as myself, but they also like to visit the pools and puddles in the lee of the bank of their own accord, simply to indulge their great love of bathing together.

37

Lapland and Snow

All among the thin-stuff shingle-stubble,
scrubby poppy-trailings and the
dirty collar tide-wrack twigs, are

Small, incessant, fidget-forage birds
mouse-managing the chinkling turnstone pebbles,
bobble-head alert along the Bank-of-Shingle skirt.

Late February winter-tinted, earth and
chalk-smudge birds, all sea-salt charcoal from a
fire-down-on-the-beach with straw-stained beaks;
Snow Buntings, sloughing off the Arctic cold with

Buntings come from Lapland – tatterdemalion with
half-rubbed-out reindeer masks for their faces,
flicker-fletched, seed husky, ermined with lemming
and rufous with rust from the rub of the year.

Common Blues

All at once, some time during the second half of summer, and always unexpectedly, the shingle bank at Salthouse bursts – not with the Sea breaking through – but with an eruption of Bird's-foot trefoil, Stonecrop and Yellow-horned Poppy, their lemon-zest brightness mitigated only by the subtle, decorators' whites of Sea Campion.

Bird's-foot Trefoil is the food plant of the Common Blue butterfly caterpillars (unremarkable little green jobs) and its widespread distribution is in large part responsible for the relative abundance of this species. An even greater claim to fame might be that – and remarkably – the wings of the adult butterfly contain no blue pigment whatsoever! Their powdery scales simply absorb every other colour of the spectrum before our very eyes, leaving us only with the blue – with a violet tinge, upon reflection.

There were so many Common Blue butterflies about on the bank this afternoon, despite the gusty wind, that I had to be careful where I was treading – and was even aware of brushing them with my knees as they clung, tight-lipped, to the metronome stems of their grasses.

This particular male (the females are actually brown with orange shelling at the edges of the wings) was turning around upon the flower head as if it were a gyroscope investigating every possible point of balance. It put me in mind, perversely, of a lorry working through its differential gears.

Bird's-foot Blues

(Polyommatus icarus)

Like flowers in the desert every seven years or so,

The toasty shingle bank is scrambled-egg yellow
and coagulating lumpy-in-the-sun with

Bird's-foot Trefoil
piling lightly at your feet –

And soon-as-bloomed, the
purse-lipped, finger-spinning wheels
are flowering themselves

With Common Blues –

Held firm against the stiff breeze
off the sea and up-and-over by the
God's Almighty Thumb and Finger
of such steeply-tumbling pea, with

Hardly weight to
spring the pollen cache, but

Every bit as heavy as an Icarus,
still tumbling from a bruised,
face turning from the Sun,
embarrassed-to-be-violent
sky.

39

Goldfinches

A flock of small birds jinking along the people-grooved ridge of the shingle bank, or suddenly rising and falling again a little way on, may not be the flurry of Snow Buntings you were hoping for. It may well be a sea-charm of Goldfinches after the very same pebble-milled seeds.

Goldfinches are an increasingly familiar garden species, doing very well just now, thank-you-very-much and turning up in goodly numbers where you might least expect them – such as here, for example. It's a win-win situation. They are the most gorgeously decorated of birds and may happily hold their scarlet, satin-faced heads up high in any avian company around the Globe. They have, not surprisingly, long been fêted and appreciated for their exquisitely delicate plumage and startling colour combination of red and yellow, black and white set on a flush-fawn background.

Elizabethans kept them in gilded cages. They even turn up in early Christian icons of Madonna and Child where the infant Jesus can be seen clutching a slightly uncomfortable looking Goldfinch as a symbol of innocence and majesty.

These particular birds were part of a much larger flock working its way through the cane-tangle jungle of Yellow-horned Poppy on the beach at Cley. They were busily pre-occupied and not at all concerned at my presence on their patch.

The trick was to try and get as many birds in focus and in interesting positions, engaged upon recognisable activities, and all in a balanced composition that is somehow pleasing to the eye. Otherwise a complete muddle might well have ensued because several of the birds had not embraced the idea of the photograph or, rather, had not been behaving themselves quite as I had imagined! Clearly, that is not the birds' priority – and thus I may or may not have succeeded.

Tangle Charm

The tangle is charmed –

The Yellow-horned Poppies all gone
and their trailings as bleached as the driftwood already –

The Goldfinches threading their
black and white, ruby-red beads,
clicky-abacus
onto the basketwork,

Snipping the craft-lesson, curly-twang lengths
with their flit-clippy, sun-slatted wings.

41

No Seals or Diving Terns

The Morston Creek
is inundated nicely. Now
the boats can ply. One

By one the people
can be handed down from
jetties, wooden-poled
into the mud. We

Are walking out on
stilts, the water
nosing at us, lifting
us with swirl and
gurgle, still. Out

Into the harbour
it is uncontained as
coffee spilled
upon a tabletop, the
mudflats left
mop only what
they can. The
tide is swollen.

Water is candlewick
and only ever slightly
corrugated. In the
Sea's mouth at the
Point, the boat turns
in the current swill,
engineless, upon a
fingertip. There
are no seals.

*'The sand eels are not
in the harbour
this year,'* says the
boatman. *'All the
seals are going
out to sea to catch them
so they haven't time
to lay about upon the
sand bank – and the
same with terns.*

*You may have noticed
none are diving here.'*
We all look round
and notice that

There are no
diving terns.

The Sand and the Seals

The sandbank heaves itself – in
one long roll, like the hardly
curvaceous back of a whale, and
glistening out of the sea.

Good and firm to pat as the
belly of a seal – and the seals
roll with it; uninspired to
heave their dead weight
into the open air, they let the

Sea deposit them, allow the
sand to come up underneath them,
lift them clear of any water,
wavelet lap-by-lap and
half-in, half-out ticklingly – and
inchingly, like horses winched from
quay to ship, their tummies in a
sling, appear. This
August the sun will

Mottle them to splattered toast, will
dry them to a sea-saw slug, their
sea-pinched nostrils and their tail
drawn up into a bow as by a
tightening string. Each

Roundly buoy-bob face
now turns to look at me
as I am standing on the
other side of all the
creek that's left and
wonders if I might be
something like a bully
Grey Seal on its end,
leftovers from the
people-boats more like
and hence I am of
no more interest. All

Afternoon they only roll under their
blubber's own momentum – one
way or the other, arbitrarily,
until the sea returns for them

And whirls them, lifts and
skirls them, fast as
any shoal of fish out to
the corners of another, much
more energetic place.

43

The Norfolk Seals

The colony of Common Seals off Blakeney Point are always a potential draw – whether you live locally and have always meant to see them, or further afield and have already pencilled them in for your next visit. Boat trips from Morston and Blakeney itself run on the tides throughout the year – though a long walk out to the Point along the Spit can be every bit as rewarding. I endeavour to do this twice a year – sometimes accompanied by one or two of the seals themselves!

Our Common Seals are not actually as common as the Grey Seals whose pups can be approached quite closely all along the beach and up in the dunes (assuming that dogs are on leads) from Horsey to Winterton around Christmas and New Year – a brilliant Boxing Day walk.

Common Seals are placid and contentedly laissez-faire creatures who don't ask a great deal of life but seem to appreciate what they do (sun, sand and sea, mostly). They always have an air of inquisitive surprise about them – well, at least in the presence of people.

Grey Seals, in contrast, are noisy, bullish and boisterous among themselves but highly entertaining for all that, the gestures and postures of the adolescents in particular quite redolent of human beings!

*The **Common Seals** rolled to a halt on the sandbanks contribute their own dark tide-wrack stripe to the familiar (though daily variegated) horizontal composition of sand, sea and sky. The texture of the darker coated individuals reminds me of the spongy sea-soaked, ancient-forest wood that is exposed from time to time, preserved along the coast towards Hunstanton, such as the Sea Henge found at Holme.*

*The **Grey Seal** pups are left by their parents to fend for themselves during the day in various states and colouration of developing pelt and are excellent subjects to photograph, being often found touchingly hugging a piece of beach flotsam, such as a plastic 2-litre milk container, as if it was a favourite toy.*

Atlantic Seal Pup

How extraordinarily unseeing (for their size) these

Oil black eyes, how new and wet, how lubricated in their sockets to turn soundlessly at me.

How un-grown into, still, this old-potato pelt, how

Unknowing of a silver slip of fish, of seaweed tangle, or a sudden blast of cold-depths current, tickly, bubbling-playful shallowness,

These hundred whiskers.

Creaky Terns

These are the noisy ones – cranking up a serious amount of floorboard creaking to keep the dusk at bay as they pour back to the Point along the shingle bank at the end of the day. These are the cocksure victims of a fashion-mugging, with their hair sticking straight out at the back – as if they've had another bad night in the dunes.

This photo has the power to transport me straightaway to that summer evening at Blakeney Point described in the poem when a Sandwich Tern hung above me for whole seconds as the incoming water filled the pool from the channel. I love the way the light has caught the beak as if it is of polished jet stone, the distinctive yellow tip to it lit up.

The Sandwich Terns

from 'The Blakeney Point'

The colony of terns
stirs up the dunes,
so far away across the sand-flats
that they wobble in the warmth – an
Irish jig or reel, a skirling seethe of them,
a salty-dry evaporation – though I
know to keep my distance;
These are Sandwich Terns and
only common where any slight
disturbance is their own. However, this is
hardly second best – I realise I am standing
in their line of flight from colony to sea,
and all they do is jink to either side of me.
I sit to let this happen properly where
creek has sculpted sand into a wishbone-
curving terrace worthy of a Gaudi
(on a plastic bag that I have
brought for underclothes).

By ones and severals the terns
materialise from what might be a
pillow-down explosion in the throng,
so sharp, so suddenly – and

Level with my knee-high cheek that
I can sense the hairs upon it rise, while they are
smoothing down the sand still further with their

Whetstone wings and
scoring doodle sand-lines
with their wingtips; others now

Returning, creaky as a
bedspring, show-off
and triumphal, almost
tapping at my shoulder
with a silver sand eel,
punchy-pleased – for
even me to see. One

Hovers, plunges at my feet
into a pool. Perhaps I am
a scarecrow seal in his mind's
eye. I see his shaggy head
(another bad-night's sleep) the
yellow tip hung with a bead of
water from his graphite beak.

I make a note beside me in the sand –
'The triumph of a sandwich tern!
One day, I'll write of it.

Drawn Lines

My tern and I
are bound to never meet
across drawn lines –

From opposite directions and
along an edgy rope of water loosened and then

Tightened – leaping clear between us,

Working up a splashy sea-green white
to keep us separate – anticipating
our close passing.

He comes jinking.
I am trying to avoid the sea
sideswiping at my feet.

I drag through shingle while he makes his

Watermark, although I notice that the waves burst to
agree his leaving, just a moment later than

They might have done.
We close and pass –
his head hung on a weight,
mine, tipped upon its jaw.

But it is he who flinches;

Now the whole sea tips from left to right behind me –

To redress a balance with the floorboard creak

Of one more mildly irritated
Sandwich Tern.

Spike Linnet

Sits prickly
and
scratched-out colourfully;

Salt-hardened spikes of silver-dead gorse
once dragged
bodily through his chest,
it seems and
broken-off and spiky in him
still, with

Bloodied pin-pricks all along the
furrows of his brow where
sea-salt dries
while
tiny grappling-iron claws
are doing battle
intricately
with these dreadful
skewer spines.

All along the cliff top are the gorse defences,
fortifying everybody like a
pike-stiletto roll of wire,
Cheval-de-frise,
deterrent
and expedient;

In all his plaintive,
up-turned,
heart-tug
elocution.

I still hear
the crisis of his conscience
for these nestlings

safe within the
blade-and-box trick of a
first-time,
an apprentice
conjuror.

Linnet Song

I personally find the plaintive, wounded and questioning notes of the Linnet's song utterly compelling and full of pathos. Sometimes, on a still and timeless summer afternoon upon the inland Heath, it can be the only sound one is aware of at all.

This male stood beautifully in profile for me atop a gorse bush with its roots in the shingle. I was taken by how the plumage seemed almost to be pricked and bloodied by the thorns as if to represent the apparently martyr-like and plainsong mentality of these little birds.

Tussocks

Every singing tussock

of this over-wintered, dried
and washed-out grass

Is a Skylark too.
A poor-man's pinstripe;

Hay and plantain plaited, raffia
and parcel-twined, pip-peppered,
seed-husk dusted – tide

marked from the wind-pricked
seep around the eyes, tie-dyed

and teasel-tufted –

'Til a bellows-worth of
tinder-catching draughts
begin to agitate a hand-fanned

Levity – and sitting pretty now,
a foot above the ground,

The Tussock bird lets go that
silo rush and trickle sound; the
music of a mile of grain still

sift and shifting – running
through the fingers
minutes later –

Only slowing up
against the side of
all the sky – to lift again, a single

Grain left up against the Sun, to

Open up the hatch once
more and simply pour and only
giving out at last upon your
own mill floor the very moment

*You forget to listen
or have lost him –*

Your own tussock head
tipped back against the ground,

Exhausted with the sound.

51

On the Possibility of such Larks being Ralph's *(for John Woodhouse)*

The cliff-top mechanisms have been wound-up and let go. The air is full of all the timely workings of Pipits and Skylarks – their up-down campanology of song.

The Lark Ascending has been on the radio this morning (it's number one on Radio FM – again), and my own inner mechanisms have been whirring with the excitations of coincidence. I wonder if these very larks were Ralph's? Ralph Vaughan Williams lived here in Sheringham for a while during 1919, in a blue and white Edwardian villa off the roundabout along the Boulevard – and surely must have strolled along the cliff-top path whilst pulling on his pipe and mulling over his music just at the point where I am often struggling for a word.

How could Ralph – forgive me, Mr. R. V. W. – he once refused a knighthood – not have been inspired by all these larks? (They still proliferate here where the grass is good and rough before the brown fields of our Green and Pleasant Land begin – so that it's hard to appreciate our national shortage.) He may have popped out for a breath of fresh sea air – it's

minutes, literally, up past the boating lake and shelter with its empty window panes – before returning to the second movement of a symphony – the Sea One, which we know he did write here. Or just to stretch his legs from having been too long at the piano, or conceivably to climb up to the coastguard hut on Skelding Hill to stand and gaze out past where there are lately wind turbines, to re-acquaint himself with something like our 'Bigger Picture'.

The answer is – apparently – that he'd already composed *The Lark Ascending* just before the outbreak of the First World War, having been much taken by George Meredith's poem – but that he did, in fact, revise it in 1920, immediately after his Sheringham sojourn – so that our Norfolk larks may well have had their belated and peculiar influence upon that final version. It's good to think of him, in any case, humming the score to himself on his way back down the sandy path, having at the very least been reminded of it by our own Sheringham birds.

Skylarks

Early summer – and the cliff top is an intoxicating place to be. The meadow grasses and the perennial vegetation between the cliffs themselves and the nearest of the arable fields are mown once an August, but left to their own devices apart from that – so their habitat is much as generations of Skylarks might remember it. This is surely Skylark City.

Because they are living so cheek by jowl, the male birds are forever engaged in trying to re-establish their pocket hanky square of territory by utilising whatever relatively high point they can sing from which will bear their weight; an already-rusty spray of sorrel, an old umbellifer spoke or even an ant-hill tuffet amongst the salt-spray thrift along the edge. Of course, they may be making an entirely vertical bee-line as presumably their real estate extends as far sunwards as their wings will carry them – though not every singing Skylark will be quite so way above one's head!

The Lark-on-a-Stick, crest raised in its excitement like an Art Deco sunrise motif, would brook no interruption to its song and allowed my clumsy approach through the waist-high, hot and toasty, insect-buzzing growth.

The bird in the pink – I almost trod upon!

Windfall of Wheatears

Windfall of Wheatears, softly
Ripe-with-migration
Apricot birds, always rolled, ever so
slightly bruised with it all – just

Out of reach.

Landfall at Salthouse where there's the
first real attempt at a proper green hill –
Out of shingle – a footfall of land before
Gamborough Hill (a hill with a name).

There are fishermen down in the roll of the beach;
I see several heads and the radio-masts of their rods.

I will sit, fisherman, too, while
April is in freefall with
sunshine and showers –
throwing a line-of-sight,
letting them come, if they will,

Though all keep a trip-and-run distance, as
Wheatears will do, to begin with;
Something, I think, of the
Swallow about them; the trimness, the
nautical fullness of throat.

There is one on a rust-wire of
Sorrel, tying a black-and-white
ticket of tail to it, clipped to a
T – fanned, to preserve its
un-tipping integrity.

New Wheatear stands barely the
stretch of a fingertip from me,

Pert as a pip, on a
salt-thick toss of the grass,
that essential Philosopher's Stone
of a light-dot in its eye; my
Mum rings on the mobile phone,
inquiring cheerily if I am somewhere
wild enough to make her glad to
be at home and counting blessings.

You call with a wee tear of your own that
I left silently at dawn, without
so much as a goodbye. I'm
sorry. I will be home soon.

Astoundingly, the Wheatear is still here.

I witness something magical.

Another film of wet cloud drags the sky, is
pulled up only thinly over shoulders and
it all goes cold again. My Wheatear

Tips his head at where the light has been.

And I have caught it.
Seen it happen.
Once in a lifetime.

This small bird's spontaneous response
to our own Sun in common –

Our un-common Sun.

55

Wheatears are one of our earliest summer migrants, passing through North Norfolk in large numbers on their way to and from their nesting grounds on the high moors and fells of northern England. Sometimes there is such a landfall of them over a day or two in mid-March or early April that the cliff tops, the shingle bank and the dunes all along the coast are inundated with them taking a brief respite and a deep breath before continuing with the last leg of their epic journey. Which is really not a problem. These are terrific little birds – the males very smartly appointed and always on the tip of their toes, which helps if you spend a lot of your time on the ground (or amongst a tumble of Lake District boulders) – both male and female infused with a delicate shade of apricot.

I'd been sitting on a plastic carrier bag at a relatively high spot at the end of the path out from Salthouse. Here the shingle bank is consolidating nicely with gorse and grass and bramble roots into proper ground that other things might grow in on just such a Spring morning, which was nevertheless a bit dicey, weather-wise, hence the bag. There were four Wheatears in good view; one male and three females. Whether they actually knew each other, I don't know. I felt sure I had taken some good photos already, but it was the magical moment when this female Wheatear actually looked up to see where the Sun might suddenly have disappeared to behind a cloud that I was most thrilled to have caught – and to have shared.

Cliff Top Kestrel

Kestrels are very much at home along the cliff tops from Weybourne to the Runtons and beyond. The shaggy grasses provide ideal hunting for them, the updrafts from the sea below the opportunity to swing their way along as if on a Sunday afternoon stroll.

The Kestrel in question in the main photograph was indeed in the close vicinity of the lifeboat station at Sheringham from where, climbing up to the coastguard hut at the top of Skelding Hill, you can very often follow the hunting fortunes of a Windhover, as these wondrous birds are quite commonly known, and get a strong sense of the intensity of concentration involved whilst standing virtually – and neck-crickingly – underneath.

I came across the second bird along the cliffs between Cromer and Overstrand – a section of coast known as Happy Valley, which was a favourite walk with Victorians who had climbed up, no doubt intrepidly, to see the lighthouse. Just here, the hunting is so good upon the tumble of gorse and scrub-colonised cliff-slippage that it is quite possible to find oneself above a hovering Kestrel with a stunning view of its rust and charcoal-splintered back. This photo was taken whilst in the company of my friend David Stapleford, the Squirrel Man, on our last walk together.

Ubiquitous (instantly recognised by most of us hanging above our motorway verges) as well as common, if Kestrels were rarer their wind-stilling exploits would no doubt be the subject of whole conservation road shows and we would flock in our hundreds to see one of the wonders of the natural world. Instead, we can be party to it any time we like. How fortunate are we?

Windhover for All

(for Patricia, with more than a nod to Gerard)

Kestrel dragnets the cliff tops
(he would pull clear everything at
once and tip it to the Sea)

Tawny tri-star way above the lifeboat station
    overlapping any lingering doubts with
throwing-out his airy hoops of
    Search & Rescue – scooting

Circles, each one bigger than the last one. Scoot –

Circling. Scoot-circling
away. He is

Playing with me;
swinging out horseshoes
'til metal clinks metal in his mind and he
makes his bright connection and is

Dropping his shoulder, butting his head on the sky with
only a nod to impatience, then
all at once falling away, yet again. He

Is working it, working it –
rubbing the shine and the glare from the
grass with his emery eye,
winnowing, tossing it high to

Separate out the root from the rootless, the
quick from the mineral dead. I

Spin while he hangs on the rim of the Sun
'til his feathers are flaring to
canvas and cork high above me.

Strings of light are looping all along the promenade
(the coloured-light bulb dolphins, crabs and giant prawns
all held aloft, religiously, at lamp-post intervals).

The Kestrel pinches swags of air together, similarly,
at his highest point – an easy, unaffected

Trinity – for vole eternities.

The wind is slipping like a gambler's counters
through his fingery wingtips; he knows
what he must lose to win. It is

The sudden lack of heart within the gale that baulks.

White-letter Hairstreaks are famously associated with Elms and their fortunes have taken a hand-in-hand tumble with the devastating effect that the Dutch Elm disease has had upon one of our most stately and quintessentially English trees.

It may seem odd to be including this highly engaging and enterprising butterfly here. But I do so because, curiously enough, one of the best places to encounter them is at the end of Lady Anne's Drive along the track that skirts the sandy Holkham Meals on its way out to the dunes, where they seem to be exploiting the suckers of elm springing up (just as enterprisingly!) around the trunks of trees that have succumbed. In this quite unlikely situation these sapling elms are struggling to reach a decent height before the effort of transpiration is just too great for the sap to rise up through the fungus-clogged capillaries. You can see that the young trees are in a bad way at the top. The butterflies press on gamely nonetheless, chasing one another round and round among the topmost healthy leaves and strolling about on their upper-sides so that when the light is right their pastry-cutter shapes can be seen distinctly from below – as if they were a shadow-show behind a leafy screen.

If you are lucky and wait long enough, then one of the White-letter Hairstreaks (the letter is in fact a sideways W) may dance all the way down through the canopy (such as it is) to drink at a bramble flower. Once it's down it may stay for a while. On one occasion, I'd been waiting at just such a bramble patch beneath an elm for about a quarter of an hour before a Hairstreak simply wandered out from behind a handful of blooms in front of my very eyes, in all apparent innocence, to try the next flower round!

This little fellow was waiting for me early one morning in July upon a bramble leaf, absorbing the weak warmth, as yet, of the Sun and drying out. He had probably been hanging on the underside of the leaf and collecting his own weight in dew overnight and was now going walkabout. The underside of his wings seems to have the bloom and texture of a potter's slip, bruised between finger and thumb.

It is the beads of dew threaded all around the edge of the leaves and all over their surface like tiny drops of blown glass that I enjoy about this photo. That – and the story it tells of a White-letter Hairstreak.

60

White-letter Day *(White-letter Hairstreaks)*

These are no more than
excuses for Elms; that
try but get so far and then
no further – gummed-up,
sap run out of worthy
green-fuse force – no
Oomph no more
against the fungus.

There is nothing for it
but for tiny butterflies who
will not yet desert them
to be whittling dead-wood
twigs down to the bone
and snappier still with
all their spinning after
one another, pole-dance
helter-skelter, down to
where it's good old
English Elm again –
though stunted, every
one along the rutted
path, a runt – still

High enough, though
(they will not come down
to brambles in this light)
for my own sap to be
thus drying-up, my head
about to die-off from its
body with an ache behind
the eyes from all this
squinting up against
the sky, the stiff neck
and the deeply-furrowed
(elm bark) brow. When

I parked-up in Lady Anne's
Drive, early, it was
tumble-weedy empty.
Now there is a horse-box,
dogs-on-leads (what else?)
and a car-boot street party
from one end to the other.

61

Knot Blown

(for Beth)

Here are knots
un-done by
a single hare,

Un-ravelled by
its shoestring
pull along the bank,

Fallen back open to the
sky – burst
mattress stuffing.

Drawn again into
a commonality as if
there were an intake of

Shared breath, or
at the very least,

A vacuum at their heart.

63

The Wash

(Knots with Standing, for The Captain and Sue)

64

All rain and bluster, the
blower full-on at the
steamed-up windows,
lights through the wipers; a
sizzling wetness under the
tyres an hour before dawn.

Last in the line of cars with their
headlamps still dying, slamming of
doors and boots, trail of us,
wordless, out to the holiday houses and
onto the wall of the sea.

For one morning only, an
'up-to-the-knees-worth' of water
is suddenly all that's required to
fill up the whole of The Wash –

With proper waves, nevertheless,
scurrying under the cuff of the wind
in this squeezing of dishwater light

And the Knots we have come for are
already heltering-skeltering
over the bank, pouring at length
from the pool, a whispered,
unravelling spool of their cotton-bud
hundreds and thousands with

One late arrival – too many at last
for the doormat of mud
left out for their feet.
The rain-sodden sky is a
burst feather-bladder of
shorebird that will not be
dampened or stuck.

And here they are –
all at once over our heads with
one tug of a drawstring that
lets them all out so we
spin on our heels at their
cumulo nimbus
that threatens to pour with
its midwinter rain, then
turns inside-out so
we've lost them again

Like midge-swarms they
blacken to fists that are
squeezing the morning and
holding it personal-close to
their dirty-snow chests; now,
shamed into lightness of
spirit, they're springing their
fingers wide open – a fly
-casting gesture for
seeding the water – to
blanket the surface
with hissings of hail.

We've lost them once more and we
look to each other to pick up the trail.

They have become inscrutable – the
single-bird-thin sheet of them is
saucer-edge elliptical, invisible, a
paper-cut across our eyes, now

Up and billowing upon a
shout we have not heard;
one cloud swing-punching
up and through another –
Bird dissolving bird,
dissolving bird…into
one saturated flock of
over-wintering Knots the
simple air cannot contain –

So they appear, no
worse for wear,

Unable, though, to keep from
gravitating into some dark
point of last-night's sky – their
own excitable Black Hole –
to be flung out again across the
knotless emptiness as if this
formless and undifferentiated
Place of Desolation were
The World's beginning.

All across The Wash
the lightening sky is
grained and gritted with them,
high and low above the
King's Lynn industries
in every innocence; a
chiaroscuro satire
on our dirty skies.

They bloom above them now –
a floating head of mushroom spores, all
nucleating daylight, then
decanting, one side to the
other of The Wash.

They're warming to this now –

Performing in their rabbit hands
behind a sheet; a
cobra-strike becomes
a leaping salmon and
a leaping salmon its own waterfall, a

slingshot hurl of shorebird
its own sling –

All unaccompanied.

The Sea has left while
we have not been looking,
trickled away like an
audience leaving,
coats over arms.

The Mud is ready for them now.

They settle out across the sky to
saucepan lids that rattle on their
rims into a frenzy with
a noise that builds and builds
until they're down –

Without a single sound.
And we are now awake and
shining of each eye with them
and with our very selves.

65

The Art of Knots

A dawn visit to Snettisham on a January Spring tide in blustery wind and rain in order to witness the incoming water squeezing vast numbers of feeding Knot onto the only visible puncture-patch of mud …until they have no alternative but to take to the sky out of the sea in one vast and single-minded shoal …is truly unforgettable… in more ways then one!

In very low light it was still just about possible to record with the camera the fluid and uncannily organic shapes that the birds were extruding and compressing from within their countless numbers. A surreal element was added by the backdrop of the Boston industries across the water, which easily confused the mind (certainly mine) into the perception that the birds were indeed just smoke.

From the hide, as the birds gather on the mud-slope shores of the inland lagoon to rest, the first sight of the undifferentiated and endless carpet of table-tennis balls of fluff that is, in fact, a flock of Knot, is one that the mind will not – cannot – readily assimilate… so that it may be some time before an individual Oystercatcher standing proud among them snaps you out of such a sense of wonder and incredulity.

As these birds rose together in front of me (apparently at concern over a hare loping along the bank), I was aware of a deep bass thrumming and then a multitude of snowy whites and greys exploding wetly on the windscreen of my lens as if it was the canvas for a wondrously impressionistic work of art. I love to draw and paint, and I am intensely aware of the idea that the interpretative aspect of our personal response to the World around us is fundamental to the very nature of Art – and yet, I cannot conceive of a way in which one might better convey the impression of 'massed flight' than by what the camera has recorded with its own eye here. Is one's response to such a photograph necessarily not of the same order as one's response to a painting that has been laboured over with passion and integrity for days or months? Interesting stuff!

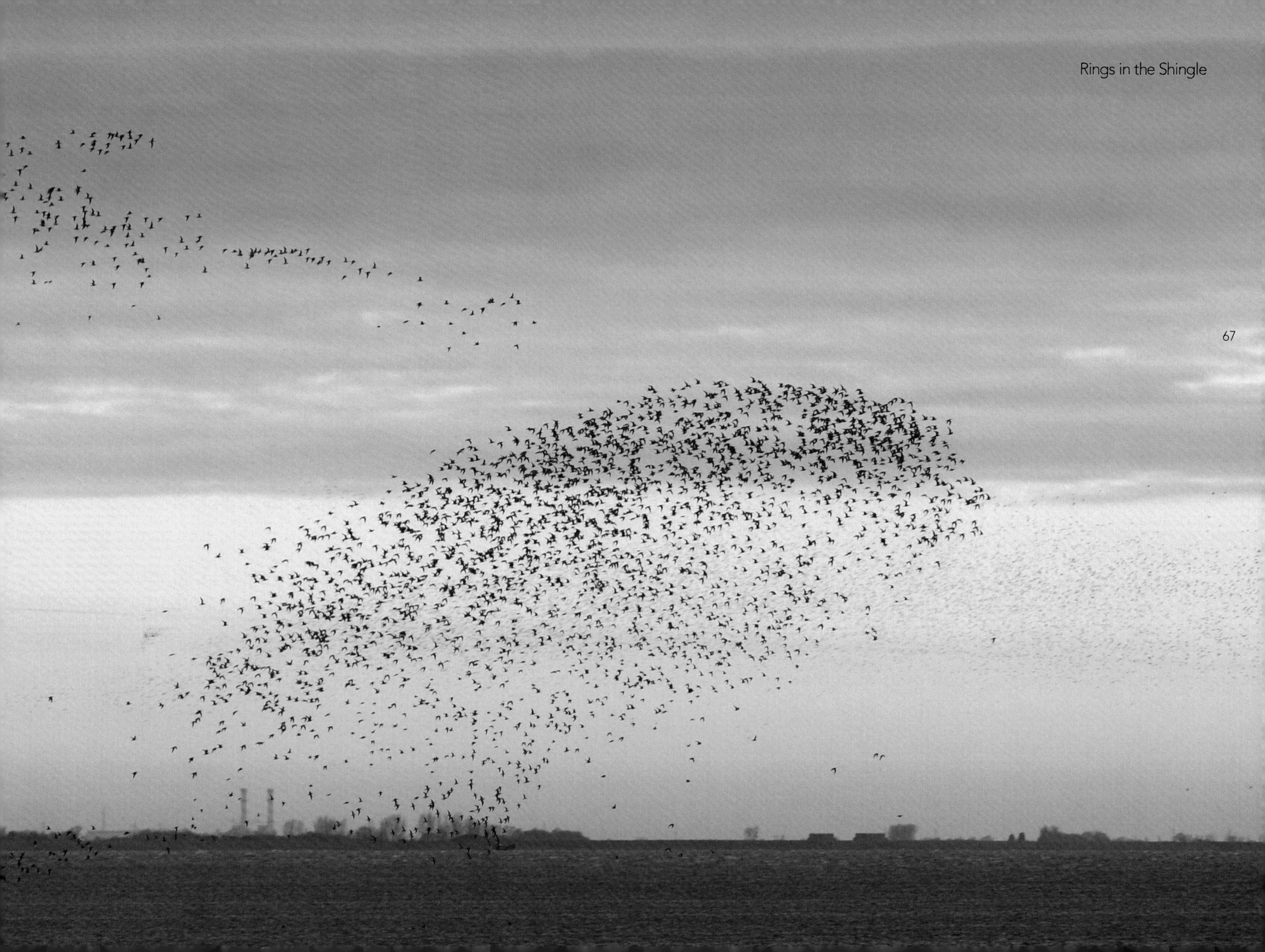

For Starlings, Read Turnstones

To quick-legged shoreline birds such as Turnstones the concrete of the seaside promenade in essence is indistinguishable from the sea-weedy, barnacled rocks and the knobbly chalk-and-flint exposures covered over and laid bare again each day by the tides. Except that is for the fact that usually the promenade is not inundated twice a day.

For such a bird a seafront promenade is simply an easy-to-get-at and interesting surface full of holes and cracks that might very well provide a home for some soon-to-be-winkled-out crustacean or insect or worm. It may or may not have seaweed or little pools to investigate. It may or may not take the form of a wide slope or steps from one level to another with a helpful and aesthetic ironwork of brightly painted railings to channel dozens of pairs of both bird and human feet or wheels at a time. That isn't really the point. The main criterion is its crumbling-and-weatheredness quality, its happy dilapidation which has encouraged its own menagerie of minibeasts. And in most popularly traditional seaside towns finding conditions such as these is no problem at all.

When I first washed up at my own particular little town of Sheringham I was astonished to discover Turnstones at almost every (forgive me) turn and every bit as much at home as any tax-paying resident; dodging and jinking between the railings and among the bare toes and skateboards of holiday-makers all along the promenade, negotiating the steep concrete slope of the cliff-retaining wall (sideways-on to come down) and offering what assistance they might to the local fishermen unloading nets and buoys on the slipway – even expecting their own fair share from the seafront garden bird tables! They seemed to have completely ousted the normally ubiquitous Starlings from this narrow and salt-spray urban niche – making it their own by sheer dint of numbers and a kind of insouciant effrontery (very much like the Starlings themselves) rather than outright aggression.

The Starlings, disenfranchised, were now contenting themselves with a backyard of pub car parks and the environs of ice-cream parlours and amusement arcades. Perched on aerials and chimney pots, they showed little sign of re-grouping or adopting anything other than guerrilla tactics. Being Starlings, and much like Turnstones, they were quite un-fazed and taking the whole thing in their pink-legged stride. (Turnstones have orange legs.)

I have become very fond of Turnstones – as indeed I am of Starlings. Whether in Sheringham town or Brancaster harbour or in the lee of the shingle bank at Salthouse, it is possible to approach within a few paces of them – always a thrill where a wild bird (or animal) is concerned – close enough to catch the tarry gleam in their eyes, as they turn a head on the end of a beak to look under a pebble or prise a shell out of the mud, or toss you a scrap of old weed high over their shoulder. Turnstones will often work a large area of shingle – or concrete – together, and one of the most uplifting experiences I enjoy is simply sitting still among them and registering the tiniest and most delicate sound I believe I have ever heard – that of a dozen turnstones doing what they do and turning stones. The intimacy of it gives me goose-pimples. It's akin to the rustle of a dragonfly's wing, the unwrapping of a sherbet lemon, or a beetle on the move (so I would imagine) beneath a crispy winter leaf.

Turningstones

Turnstones are giving
everyone-the-runaround –
feet for the feet and
anybody's guess.

Wearing
'Am I Bothered?'
T-shirts for the
Seafront concrete
or the slipway shingle,
promenade at length or
tide-bump boulders –

No more opportunist
or no less than
all the jolly rest.

Beneath our plastic slap
and happy-hubbub crowd, the
Sea's recycling roar,

The turnstones
jumble-rummage
ceaselessly, examining
forensically and
undistractedly – and

with a chinkling
understatement far
outside our
holiday capacity
to pick out from the
gull and ice-cream
scenery, they

Tinily and
Easily and
Left to be,

Turn the
World over
To see.

I like this photograph for its contrast of textures – the concrete, the muted softness of winter plumage, the rust – as well as its odd juxtaposition of containing lines and of course for its turnstone, looking out over the edge, with (as ever) an eye for the main chance.

Brambleby Books

Other Nature Books by Brambleby Books

Norfolk Wildlife – A Calendar and Site Guide
Adrian M. Riley
ISBN 978 1908241 047

British and Irish Butterflies - The complete Field, Identification and Site Guide to the Species, Subspecies and Forms
Adrian M. Riley
ISBN 978 0955392 801

Birds Words – Poetic images of wild birds
Hugh D. Loxdale
ISBN 978 0954334 734

Arrivals and Rivals – A duel for the winning bird
Adrian M. Riley
ISBN 978 0954334 796

Garden Photo Shoot – A Photographer's Yearbook of Garden Wildlife
John Thurlbourn
ISBN 978 0955392 832

Winging it – Birding for Low-flyers
Andrew Fallan
ISBN 978 0955392 856

Never a dull Moment – A naturalist's view of British wildlife
Ross Gardner
ISBN 978 0955392 870

Buzzing! Discover the poetry in garden minibeasts
Anneliese Emmans Dean
ISBN 978 1908241 078

Birduder 344 – A life list ordinary
Rob Sawyer
ISBN 978 1908241 092

And listen to the Waves – Selected Poems
Brian Churcher
ISBN 978 1908241 191

Making Garden Meadows – How to create a natural haven for wildlife
Jenny Steel
ISBN 978 1908241 221

Sheer Cliffs and Shearwaters – A Skomer Island Journal
Richard Kipling
ISBN 978 1908241 214

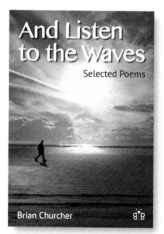
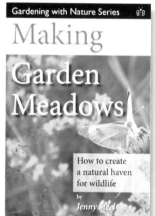